Cane, Corn
& Gully

Safiya Kamaria Kinshasa

Out-Spoken Press
London

Published by Out-Spoken Press,
Unit 39, Containerville
1 Emma Street
London, E2 9FP

A CIP record for this title is available from the British Library.

First edition published 2022
ISBN: 978-1-7399021-2-4

Typeset in Adobe Caslon
Design by Patricia Ferguson
Printed and bound by Print Resources

Out-Spoken Press is supported using public funding by the National
Lottery through Arts Council England.

Supported using public funding by
ARTS COUNCIL
ENGLAND

Contents

skin is missing

'For what can poor people do, that are without Letters and Numbers, which is the soul of all business that is acted by Mortals, upon the Globe of this World.'

— *Richard Ligon, Barbados, 1657*

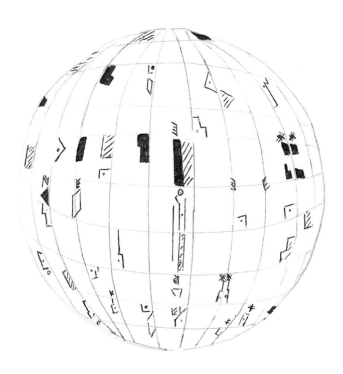

— Ms Abennah (1715), Ms Gabriela (1954),
Ms Nadine (1997)

Phrase 18

Notes:

liberation & violation
usually ends de same way:
lying on a merciless surface
exposed, unclean & hungry,
yuh DNA loss
on another deserter,

there need not be
a choreographer for dis part
here, nobody teach we tuh swallow
our hearts every morning
but here we are,
with phantoms drinking tea
in our skulls

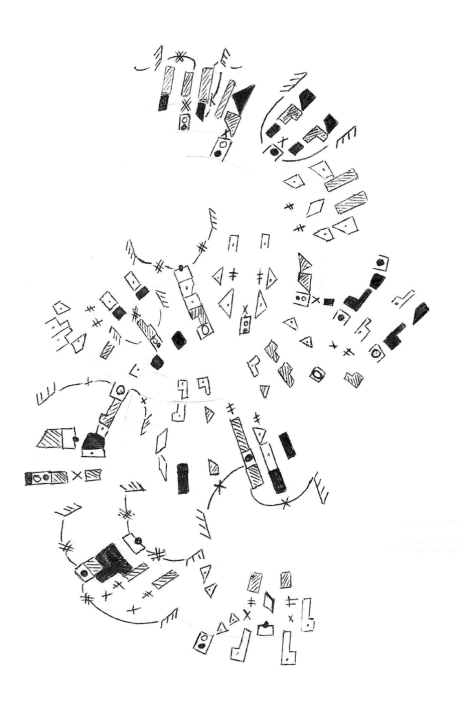

3

I Tied My Teeth to My Feet & Ate My Own Testament

a man broke my grandmother's jaw with headlice
she turned tuh sweetgrass & goatskin
i squashed my fingers in my stomach stuffed in a bucket
got better at sacrificing tings
my hands hung in Porter's stable
wore cornrows & creole
so no one noticed my eyes were inside out
even my family never knew which way to bury me
i will forget
                              i will remember my family
                  who did not know in which direction to hug
                  my neck skipped alongside a double decker
                              wore deep wave & perm
                      tossed pop music across Charlton Park
                          became brilliant at stealing myself
                  unzipped my tracksuit pickpocketed my brain
                  the rest of my mouth is stored in a sack ah yam
                          breaks apart the mother i break

Bone & Breathless

in 1905 i lay on a ground who also gasped fuh water
dis ground   made room fuh me inside its stomach
den asked de sky if it could collect me
meanwhile an ant hunted my leg fuh a sky

in 2017 a wind behaved like a newly divorced man
sucking on toe knuckles & other lewd parts
again   i lay on a ground
dis time with soca engulfing my lungs
as i gasped fuh air de ground   again
asked de sky if it could claim me

de ground has never seen daylight on its back
so why wouldn't it ask day fuh permission tuh take me
when i panting cruel & cut

my dark & gender been hauled like a spider & puncheon
leaving trails ah cassava juice & boiling fish-liver oil
soon i will grapple a day's neck with my thighs
bring it to de state it was before God called it 'good'

                        leh we all be equal & hideous

De Wind Only Likes Me From de Waist Down

St. Andrew, Barbados, 1790 / Christ Church, Barbados, 2003

my vagina is a machete

last time i see massa

de wind grab my skirt   lift it up & up

massa cartwheel over

dere are too many branches on de trees

dat is de biggest quarrel wunna have

should ask de wind tuh flog dem

so de last one sing calypso

not allahwe haunted

not allahwe frowsy in wunna mess

massa fuzz-out with pigs

before wheeling tuh my skirt

he peenie ting ova yonda

he thumb back by de octopus bush

                      up & up it goes

The Casuarina Tree Is an Elder

St. Joseph, Barbados, 1848–Present

when i was worth a horse,
i escaped in a seagull's mouth,
a canon shot it down into a stream,
for six days i remained hidden in its beak,
until de stream offered me a new grave,
today, children roll me in their games,
they practice leaping & dodging,
i prefer this life, for who was my spirit then?
but a woodlouse feeding on a rotting family,
at least this time i can be there,
when de children's laughter curdles into foam

Small Breasts & Sweetcorn

blessed with bounties that ain't given much attention
i give them the affection they deserve,
spend all the hours there are in minutes
stripping husks & fine hairs,
once gave all i had to a new island breed,
he wiped my legacy with his sleeve then left
give me love or give me oblivion

he met me cocooned in loose cotton,
nipples high & willing,
he swished me in his mouth like hop-weed,
we planned to ride a donkey between stars & turnpikes,
until i was replaced by a new her
a heavy breasted more capable of service her,
i was too much of old God, drought & gully,
i made wine from his ribs
give me love or give me oblivion

between me & fugitive me there is always a mother
explaining 'simple' ain't nutting to be ashamed of,
attention gets you left by the reeds
with your legs separated from your name
& even then some like em scrawny, easier to pull.
i love eating my indecent corn with the husks removed,
my bare unbothered crops
give me love or give me oblivion

Phrase 4

Notes:

woman in field	woman in house	woman in church
woman in alley	woman in labour	woman in mouth
woman in egg	woman in bed	woman in ditch
woman in land	woman in tea	woman in ocean

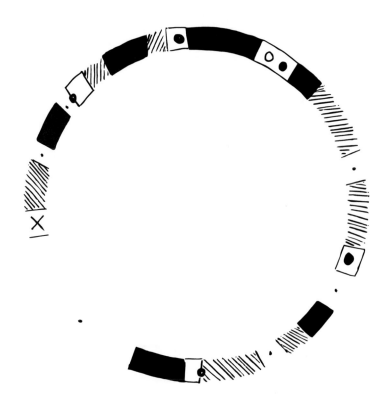

Flying Fish

St. James, Barbados, 1813

i was snipping off fins when muh water break
dere are too many bones in us tuh be breeding
we should be more fish   why not grow scales
i noticed its mouth wide & ready
                i wanted tuh finish scraping de guts
it needed tuh know it was dead

when i released muh daughter her mouth was shut
doing whatever de hell she wanted
 covered in belly   her grandmudda hung she
upside down   smacked she boxcy   i heard she cry
dere are too many brains fuh us
               tuh be doing de same ting

i never finished soaking muh peas
i might just pretend tuh sleep so i don't have tuh
  a cock is being erected in St Michael
a thanks fuh saving lives
                 i begat one   aunty begat three
                    so where de ass is we statue?

perhaps i can borrow a fisherman's hook
hide it in muh basket   take a trip tuh town
swing at de statue   bag Mr Lord up in quarter pounds
sell he at market   or exchange he fuh more fish

I Am Doing the Best I Can

i saw a wood pigeon hop off a bus,
i think it's the smartest living thing on this island,
we work too hard, we should be beating ice-cream
at midday, we should be using our knees
for more productive activities. have you noticed
we stand in prayer like we are waiting for a bus?
have you seen a wood pigeon do it?
i mean pray, it just stands there
like it knows the bus is coming but doesn't care
if it comes because it's made up its mind
it will not fly right now. imagine
having the audacity to say having knees
doesn't mean you have to beg & having arms
doesn't mean you have to make a living for anyone
but yourself. when i uproot our yams
i poke my fingers in the earth deeper,
to feel if she birthed more, i wonder if it hurts her,
if my fiddling & hoping for more makes her feel invalid.
does she know what dirt is? everything giving is ugly.
a woman with a nice car watched me miss the bus,
she kept driving. my hugs are getting longer,
i appreciate the way the dip in your shoulder tastes:
an uncharted ravine for sweat no one else can have.
we have enough food for a week.
the pigeon had a nice demeanour, i will give it a name

I Salted de Mud With My Palms but More ah Me Grew

St. John, Barbados, 1649

i spent nuff time telling young cane i was not born
cutting my way through a snake:
de stalks call me a monster
cause my kin & i forced to hack at dem chests,
de young cane say dem know dey is supreme
cause dere are so many ah dem now
so i tell dem no, no young cane,
more ah you doan mean nutting
& dem tell me no, if you keep getting cut down
& keep growing yuh mussie mean someting,
so i tried tuh convince young cane i is not a jumbie:
bushels ah water stomp my eyes,
i have thrown cane onto a cart
after seeing my brudda remove de same way,
if i hang myself tonight,
tomorrow i will be back in de field
hundreds ah me to de left
to de right front back
every diagonal above below,
when young cane reaches maturity it grows a thick shell,
only when you break its neck
is when you hear it hiss de resurrection song

What More Do You Expect From a Woman Whose Hands Are Made From Okra?
St. Peter, Barbados, 1661

everything back then could be cured
with a difficult parable because people
just enjoyed de sound of a confident answer,
that used to be enough

one day a clay-tempered girl
asked a no-nonsense woman *why?*
de woman gave instructions for how to scrub
a Triton's trumpet, over time everyone forgot
de original question, then 'how to scrub
a Triton's trumpet' became de only answer

then everyone forgot what needed cleaning,
now all we are left with is 'how to scrub',
no one wants to be naked,
someone may confuse cowskin carols
drawn across your back
with a clumsy accident,
then laugh

Behind de Garrison
St. Michael, Barbados, 1975, 1795

if your pomp & pageantry
were to be hunted like a rat
who mutilates crops,
every man swaddled
in blue & red cotton
might learn he is unkillable,
her majesty rocked you
with bullets she called you
hers before i did,
when de general bought your
dignity he saw hammocks
on your nostrils, he lost too
many men fighting de heat,
when he made you watch over
us you became his lavender oil
he slept
but you never slept again,
your unthinkable thoughts
congregate by my chest behind
de garrison
we acclimatise to its purpose
become barbaric beneath de
bushes, i hear cannons in your
legs, i know you want more
but ain't nutting between these
thighs a flag will surrender to,
so, we both gonna have to find
another way to win a war
where we don't have to play
dress up you look ridiculous
we both do i was hoping you
could undo de   shame

inside my throat but i failed
to unbind de knots in your
head, we will just have to do
it in costume, here,
near de armoury maybe a
gun will overhear us
speaking in tropics & show
us what de crown failed to
preach

Sometimes Death Is a Child Who Plays With Rubber Bands

a torn sistah mastered folding her cervix into her purse
     on the fourth day of burnings she mastered this —
it was a magnificent time for learning new skills,
  we asked de field crickets to teach us,
               to lay eggs without wings,
      never give your child an inheritance it cannot use,
you can never be too sure when it might be snatched.

we must stay low & positive, sing.
morning cannot wipe the sweat from our brows,
     it rises like a mother & like a mother
                  it will eventually leave.

 de worst is coming, wicked as dawn,
 it has passed the border between de patty shop & casino
smelling like spring's death & whored-out candles.

we gambled all our wishes on dandelions,
now we celebrate de little tings
       every unburnt rice grain & regrown eyelash
vaulting between lemon vines & dog friendly cafés.

      just because we do what needs to be done,
it doan mean we nah ready, we just aware
  there are too many of us to be martyrs

Preface: And if by Some Miracle

It was my fifth night terror in a row. I woke in an ocean of sweat and dribble with my thighs burning from running through mahogany trees, cane fields and the bloodcurdling ancestors' screams. Prior to this, I was researching the Trans-Atlantic Slave Trade; although the horrors have never felt less repugnant to read, the void of first-hand narratives from enslaved people (particularly women) was more infuriating than usual, especially now I was reading as a poet. Sometimes I traced texts just to find an utterance, but they were not speaking. And to my devastation, I could not find a single word from an enslaved woman in Barbados. It was my fifth night terror in a row, and I felt myself succumbing to the abyss.

I left the ocean for dry wood, I shook my torso, my fists and stomped my feet. I spread my fingers, stretched my arms to the ceiling, lunged on a diagonal pointing my left toe as far as it could crawl. My hips liaised with the chill from my window, my right knee joined in and a conversation between me and fugitive me began. The discourse lasted for roughly thirty minutes before I realised being able to speak through movement is as much 'inheritance' as it is 'talent'. I immediately browsed through every description I could find of an enslaved person moving (at 2 o'clock in the morning). I discovered the enslaved were speaking, constantly.

One woman shook her head while gagged with iron, another made circles with her arms in the cane field as the sun rinsed its heat over her, with her baby wrapped around her back. And, after being flogged to the ground another woman beat the ground with a rhythm of her own. These fleeting descriptions were of course obscured beneath a colonial gaze; however, I was certain if I focused on the fundamental actions, I could loosen the gaze whose teeth marks can be found on my own anatomy. I decided to embody as much as I could to write my nation back into history.

The work is dangerous; writing into history is like feeding unknown seeds while attempting to control the rate of their growth. Sometimes when I danced, I inhaled the language of my ancestors' captors, and they became mine. So, I made the following decisions:

-   The collection only features motifs which are still present today in Barbados and/or performed by a descendant.

-   The word '~~dance~~' is absent from the collection: every action/breath is a part of the grand choreography.

-   The word '~~Black~~' is absent: '~~Black~~' only exists because '~~white~~' dictated '~~Black~~' was '~~Black~~', but if '~~Black~~' was asked for its name it may have said 'Ɔdɔ', or 'Ẹlẹwa' or 'Damn Fine'.

-      The word 'body' is absent: the land and person
       may share the same voice.

-      In African diasporic dances, preservation and
       evolution usually happens concurrently: by the
       time you finish reading this note there will be
       another variation of 'the whine' in conversation
       with the original movements. Therefore, time is
       not linear in this collection.

I travelled through reports and letters from the 1600s, to
       modern churches, to limes, to kitchens and even
       market stalls. Sometimes I observed as a
       bystander, sometimes as a participant, harvesting as
       many testimonies as I could, tucking them between
       my cornrows.

I cannot tell you how to think or feel about my work,
       nor can I force you to recognise every 'Kitoko'
       member of my ancestry deserves a dignified burial,
       but, if by some miracle you can acknowledge my
       nation has always been speaking, then maybe they
       can finally join in the discourse of their narratives.

Gully

Riding the bacterium causing tonsilitis in William Wilberforce's throat,
1689, 1789

a, red, and, whip, man, strip, a, gul, ly, from, my, gul, let,
my, voice, would, run, dat, way, tru. tru. tru, de, mud, de,
gunk, when, mas, sa, came, he, came, at, night, he,
would, press, his, choke, tuh, my, ear, i, was, a, low, tide,
i, tried, tuh, hack, his, his, what, do, you, call, dis, part,
ah, man, dat, em, balm, me? my, toe, nails, grew, night,
fall, my, hole, wide, ned, as, he, punched, with, his, with,
his, liz, ard, tast, ed, like, brine, my, voice, ran, but, ne,
ver, get, far, it, tried, tuh, jump, off, de, edge, ah, east,
but, he, al, ways, find, it, vis, its, me, ag, ain, and, steals,
an, ud, dah, gul, ly, his, his, his, his, sho, vel, bit, de,
right, side, ah, my, neck, my, knuc, kles, lob, bied, ag,
ainst, de, dig, ging, but, im, go, deep, in, my, rib, den,
strip, my, gul, ly, like, im, strip, my _ my,
sir, you, claim, tuh, want, all, ah, we, wid, dout, we, soft,
parts, bound, up, in, a, cart, but, you, say, man, say, man,
say, man, say, man, say, man, ag, ain, im, make, hol, low,
un, der, my, blouse, i, shrunk, seek, ing, and, push, ing, i,
am, sure, i, made, a noise, i, doan, tink, wun, na, heard,
or, yuh, heard, but, doan, know, what, i, said, i, said,
, , , i, said , , , , , , , ,
, , , , sir, can, you, re, peat, what, i, said?
wid   me   crouch   ing   in
your   gul   let

Hungry Man

a knotted man with nutting in his bowl
swallowed de north star   de whip & de queen
hope tasted foul   oppression had nuff soul
he ate de thunder   God's wrath was too clean

he chomped on de deck who bore his hunger
wild-tooth geckos studied him as a runt
baptised in bile he choked on de flavour
dived in a dead lamb to steal a new gut

it was too late he could no longer eat
de queen raised an army in his spirit
white horses & guns bolted from his spleen
no north star but de cowskin came flying

hungrier folk watching picked up their bowls
flung dem at de queen shouting we want more

('we want more' – repeat until de screaming
builds enough friction with de Queen's army tent
& catches fire)

We Coming

chip & chip away to bear fruit

break boulders so stubborn in de gap

curling up de spine like is a pig tail

spread luk a ackee tree leh we ball up

mashing up de road tuh bring we troubles down

shuffling a frenzy taking back de town

riots in de street police wanna fight

bloody feet sweaty body protect de standpipe

jab jab devils got chains fuh yuh guns

Jamballassie got rope fuh yuh son

Mudda Sally ready boa she dun sobbing

all de women dun tear dere stockings

yuh vex when you see we getting on bad

we gine take anudda road den de whole island

The Devil Can't Two-Step

de storm   began   in my   knee-caps
by the   time it   grovelled   to my   feet my
neck was   too sore   to greet   danger
he strolled   in on   pointe in   tights said
he did   not want   me to   seize up
de air   was not   sturdy   enough
to grip   dragged me   to de   centre   by my
cornrows   clapped &   stomped his   sharp hoofs
i was   sick by   de   abomination
his lack of rhythm
was disorientating cawbleh wat a jackass
i was forced to make my own beat
he stopped in envy
de courtship between my legs & i improved
started with a two-step
we always start with a two-step
i began charting a new constellation
zig-zagging criss-crossing shuffling hoofing
de galaxy ain't Greek
launched my spine
de rhapsody formed
my spoiled back sugared de sun
limbs graced every continent
where my eyes used to levitate
& de world was mine
he didn't like that

when he got close enough
i jump-split on his straight nose
crushed it with two million jumpers
heard a crack his nostrils flattened
he screamed like ungreased iron
i opened *my mouth*
displayed *my teeth*
pressed deeper to smother him to death
with my sister's death
with my aunty's death
all de deaths every lady had to
squeeze between her legs
then two-step like nothing happened

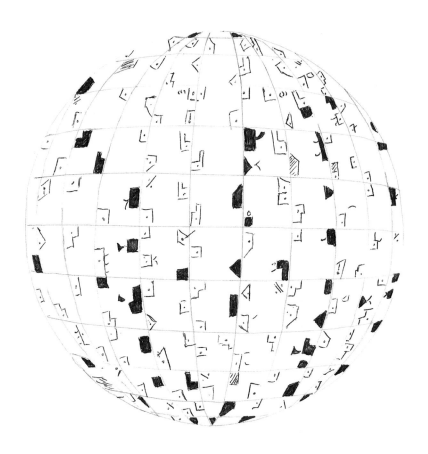

he pleaded with me to stop, i told him

no no, that's not how this works
you demanded my body,
now take it.

They Lived. That Was Enough

Quashie
Sankoh
Tambah
Banah
Senah
Dido
Adela-
mah
Nana
Lara
Konta
Michael
Gamba
Kemba
Law-
rence
Wadele
Ayo
Miri
Dami
Brian
Jane
Tabitha
Jaleel
Herbert
Olusola
Agom-

bah
Sade
Yawa
Amina
Kwaku
Phillipa
Abbo-
bocah
Komah
Nayjah
Selena
Shane
Beatrice
Sally
Leon
David
Rambo
Gibbar
Ikemba
Kaelem
Peal
Gabriel
Nancy
Seesa
Bako
Appa
Ohye-

fenah
Precious
Abenah
Kojo
Andrew
Wanita
Sinai
Tyrese
Simon
Banna
Jaja
Abigal
Jennifer
Thayoo
Ekemma
Onogo
Marwa-
rye
Myriam
Quabe-
dah
Addae
Tamisha
Cujoe
Thomas
Iysha

Arinze-
chukwu
Luke
Okoro
Eliza-
beth
Alison
Abel
Jasmine
John
Betty
Marga-
ret
Fanny
Thomas
Alisha
Henry
Clyde
Gwen-
dolyn
Ingrid
Arthur
Kojo

Phrase 57

Guest Choreographer:

The Bearded Fig Tree

Notes:

when you are not able to bury your roots
you must remain vigilant
& become de prayers you offer

Excerpt from *A True and Exact History of the Island of Barbadoes*

'These negroes have no religion…'
— *Richard Ligon, 1657*

i believe rum-bullion takes too good a liking to me,
since watching these negro women i have become
unwell, them, who hide drums in pineapple carcasses.
i grow more delirious by the day, the doctor says
it is the heat, he knows little, he has not gazed
upon the grimaces in their backs, they make mischief
at night, they splinter holy trinities with their waists,
the sun, believe my word it did not leave
the eleventh hour for two days, my lips were roasted
between a psalm, i stopped reading midway
when i saw a new-moon girl parading like boiling peas,
i smelt roses as she pivoted among the stench of them,
THEM. i wanted her to spin more: to give
me a countryside singing barley with greenfinches.
i may never return home, the wheat is dry
across all parishes, yet soursop trees grow on the east
side of their houses. all my eyes cannot be trusted,
what women are these who cackle with their pelvises
                              thrusting thrusting thrusting
they will make totems with my hair. their nakedness.
what heaven would take pickaninnys?

                    i am hungry & too afraid to eat

A Mother in Israel
St. Michael, Barbados, 1824

you should pray like you shoot, with your mouth scrunched,
             i built my first church in my house
       not knowing if a psalm could survive with firearms.
       when i say i built my first church i mean i made space
             inside myself, the same way dusk sweeps
         a gecko under its toenails. my second church
was humble: my congregation didn't mind praying behind
         laundry, i trimmed excess hair from sermons,
      preaching what the congregation shouldn't do which
         English priests did before service started, i would
    never be a hypocrite. tell someone not to do what i ain't
       planning on doing, i will do it. we do not all serve
       the same God, some gods are literate: they will read
       the shaking in your hands when you hear a bloodthirsty
       gospel about how paradise must be clean from you.
    the mob will begin their hunt soon, they know my scent,
          they say i have mongrelised blood because my hair
can grow the length of an axe and part like a bloated wave.

Testimonial From Castor Oil Girls Who Still
Found Rainbows After

we pulled ourselves out of bins after being smeared on
grown men's thighs   grown: strong enough
to overpower with little force   we know all slime
some can make your chest ashy
we traded our ears for safety nets   when vicars pressed hail
marys into our cheeks we caught acne
we buckled our knees while drilling gills in our knickers &
fins in our bras   we accepted what might happen   we did
all we could to prevent it   we promise romance
don't live   between our legs
we got room for   everyone but us
we cut cornrows   from our resumes
& publish doctr   ine with our curves
we don't unbutton   our necks cause
we got schoolwork to do
we are studying prisms
how they become spectacular
after intrusion

12 Shots Who Warned Me 'Sweet' Was Dangerous

12. i first witness a shootin at a corner shop. i was five.
heard men carvin tantrums outside den *BANG!*
   cashier gone street gone — jus a man lyin
                       widdout a pillow.
       i approach de fella, ask if he was okay
but de man was so transfix on de sky,
     he neva mine he life drainin down a pothole,
        i was too fraid tuh see what he was starin at.
no one was around tuh explain wa appen
so i walk back tuh my elders alone widdout my sweets.
i need a hug most ah de time now.

        11. whenever de ice-cream van song play i
would quarrel wit my stamina
         tuh run quicker tuh de van,
but every stinkin day my Bico Sandwiches
      were outta stock.
den one day, mid-song mid-run *BANG!*
   police say he was fillin de cones wit crack.

10. mosquitos did not suck fuh two weeks after a man
who sniff crack lick me —

    he took he shot. i became aware ah de gaps i had,
& de gaps i wanted.
        9. i was sixteen years old
when i started lovin de sound ah de ball escaping
from de iron tunnel, a fella i liked neva miss a shot.
second time i watch he play,
     he took me back tuh he house.
neva ask me tuh watch again. was neva my game.

8. now dis man in de club had no game whatsoeva —

couldn't unstan de word *no*.
    i was eighteen when i try an beat he wit a shot glass.
                      7. da same night i salute Sean Paul
wit gun fingers ready tuh pull de trigger
                            if he diluted de sun — he did.
        was it so wrong fuh me tuh ask fuh a Jamaica
so thick it was a Xaymaca
                   dat would need tuh be stop an search
                         before enterin de club?
i ben my hand — squint my eye an *BANG!*

6. *violence is not de answer:*

when i was eight dis was de sermon ah de day,
        durin communion i suggested better tastin wine
knowin nobody cud beat me.
a clergy member shot me a scorn — dat scorn was enough.

5. same week, i shot a scorn at a white woman who push
gran gran in de supermarket. dat scorn was not enough
shudda kick a grapefruit at she head. *clean up on aisle
five.* **4.** dere is no need fuh drama.

an de shot mummy catch ah me squeezin de life outta
teddy when i was two proves dis - only de need tuh
protect wunna kin. or **3.** yourself.

  de year i met my father was de same year
                 a Bajan man use a cricket bat on me.
tried tuh claw my way out im breath.

i scream fuh mummy. i scream fuh kindness.
my head catch glass
            an wit glass i exile nuff manhood tuh escape.
shud ave gone fuh de jugular. shud ave tekken dat shot.

2. sometime after dat i went into exile. do you know wat
it means tuh pull a country from yah chest tru yah neck?
                        walk widdout a home believin
you is a good fuh nuttin girl?
                    a betta man ask fuh a shot dat same year
but i was still holin de las. **1.**

        in 1994 Tropical Storm Debby fire a warning shot
in a cloud. de odda clouds jus kep movin like dey ain
care dem cud get hurt.

dey are wat dey are, an i always admired dem stamina.

G.O.A.T.

Ms Mavis is talking to an oil drum

now a fig

bats are having seizures in her hair

she is fiddling with hot pepper sauce

as if it is the handle of the house she robbed

it was her house

now she is talking to Adia

this is not suspicious because

Michelangelo hated cornflakes

his clothes looked like his bellybutton

he stabbed someone

but he refused to eat cornflakes

one day he stole a fresh clementine

he got away with it

he discovered it is okay to be more pith than muslin

it is okay to smell like swordfish

when you can draft God in a bonnet

I Am Holding the Mona Lisa Hostage Until You Return My Fourth Great Grandmother

i wanted a father to hug me very tightly
to play pattycake buy me fabrics to make Imani dolls
who had daddies too   daddy's gone west   the rum shop

opens at eight am his mama took a switch
to his cheek as a boy for leaving   she switched
him for another fella who looks like a daddy i wanted

loyalty is illogical i see this now
the acts which begat power begat me at some point
a woman had a child stolen who had a child stolen who

had a child in-between a wife's legs asking
                                        to be born again
reparations are for freedom   freedom is a lie

honour my crime   first with a woman
swollen from her ankles in grief
wrapped in reeds   make the clock's hands crawl

                                        backwards open
its stomach   you have prayed so lazily
lit candles for a woman with no eyebrows

your woman could never   could never
boil sorrel leaves yet you called her angel
serenaded her with selfies

                        i will live today

39

sacrifice a bull if you must
use its horns to calculate longitude
hold a freshly lit cigarette to Mickey Mouse's grin

i really don't care just get it done

I Laid Flowers on His Grave Then Waited fuh Him on de Veranda

i learn tuh use a fan cause de sun turn blue-eyed
watchin dutiful daughters bored on de steps. dem knot
dem knickers into jack in de boxes, out jump a screamin
clown. i was too young tuh learn how tuh do dis but not
young enough tuh learn tuh wait fuh a great man tuh
return. one lady sat fuh suh long cawblehn her eyes
could catch mongoose, she stare beyond her steps fuh
one hundred & thirty-nine nights widdout blinkin.

we would fan our necks like fresh fish cakes, tell ghost
stories & make dolls from grass, cotton & tea-bags.
we played high-born, stole imaginary men from each
odder. young belly women are lusted fuh. road men wi
hot wings on dem lips rest dem eyes on de dumplings
between our legs. when granddaddy lef, he fuhget he tie
so i figure he would come back an protect me.

my granddaddy's face evacuated first. i was de only one
in de room holdin he hand as a shadow of a man stared
back. a labyrinth rose across he mouth, maybe dat is why
he get lost & my face ain de kind dat got a future.
perhaps i am a burden fuh havin expectations fuh what is
mine bein return. or i have become too english believin
people can belong tuh me.

i live in de potholes between clasped fingers & nets.
you might find me slippin on de pavement when i think

i see someone who might look like dem won't go missin.
i study turtles with dem eggs. buried, den emergin
& goin de right way widdout a guide. yes, i dream,
yes i is over yonder. a girl will bury herself in de horizon
if she sees a return in him.

Phrase 41

Guest Choreographer:

The Ship

Notes:

freestyle is not as free as people think it is,
you are still controlled by your environment,
try not to think too much.
remember to maintain your integrity
before you find a safe place to empty
a mother's screams

*

- 'falling' can be 'rising'.

- maintain contractions when turning.

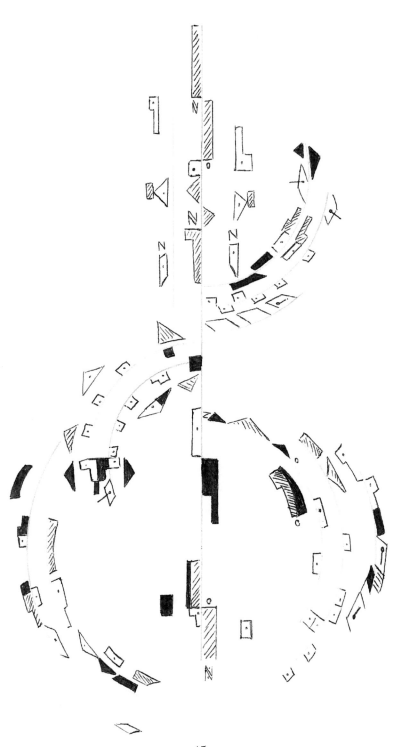

Across-Atlantic Child

when was de last time you arrived at yourself
                                  & wanted to stay?

i once watched de whole Nativity
                        three wise men passed each other
                de police came

  de police stayed longer than de donkey
i lied   i didn't watch it all

  my adolescence tasted like February
                      when pelicans were suspended

            mid-migration

  & couldn't figure out if they left for de right reasons

foreign surveyors grazed on my first village
                     they offered money
de way kids encourage each other to fight

  de village took up knitting
        crocheted new belly-buttons for their offspring

       i was delivered seven hundred & five places

everything i own is nothing i have
  no bed or couch or street can locate my birthmark

       i dreamed i was cradling frightened carrots

                              a bush evaporated
            cricket song grew stronger than my breath

       mama & i ended up on a tired trampoline
                                 if i could i would have
      bounced high enough i would have

          hurled myself into a streetlight
                    made all my uncles be at de right time

      i passed myself eating flying-fish cutters on a fountain
                              pelicans studied rest
              a blue-haired uncle sat next to me
      asked if i could float

Pork/Interlude

Elmer J. Fudd dropped a bomb on Bugs Bunny
who strolled out unscathed, waving through the smoke,
Elmer couldn't decide whether to drop another bomb
or wave back. i don't eat red meat,
i waved away pork but the waiter still dumped pigtails
on my plate. All language is irresponsible.
i was in a guava field,
doing exactly what you do in a guava field,
a farmer enjoyed my waxing gibbous cheeks
& the way i squashed fruit inside of me —
he assumed i would enjoy digesting his stories
which got me thinking about what strobe lights
i should buy for my casket,
perhaps i should perform no gesture at all
& just stay dead. Elmer made a decision,
he pulled out his gun, a marshmallow exploded
in my hot chocolate, i think life would be very boring
if we kept it all in the same mug,
Porky Pig appeared stuttering *th-th-th-that's all folks*
like he knew this ick wouldn't be over any time soon

Phrase 63

Guest Choreographer:

The Afro Comb

Notes:

it's not about being upright & cute
you gotta keep it raw & real
lead from the base all the way to the tips
your feet Genesis your fists Revelations

remember to hit the 'and'
after you spin
and one and two AND bap bap
like that

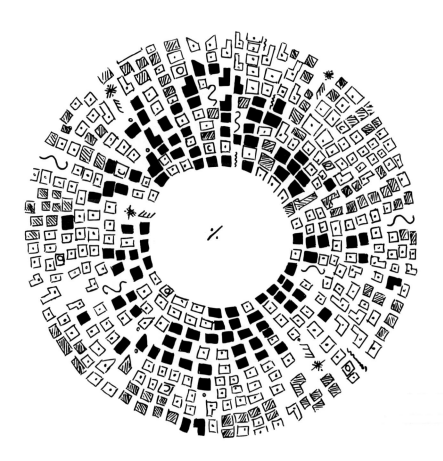

Our Culture Came of Age & Grew Nipples for the BBC & Hollywood to Suck On
London, England, 1974

a woman juggled her titties censored in coconuts
she wore a grass skirt   her face was smoked
not sauced like mine   more Fred Astaire's rhythm dark
her lips were
Benin-statue-got-uprooted-from-them-blood red
she had a penis   she was six-foot-tall
a fruit basket balanced on her poorly tied headwrap
i sat by the mangoes   there was nowhere else to sit
the mangoes were uncharacteristically hostile
like what did she do to make those mangoes so mad?
the audience hacked up Caribbean islands to make stars
tossed them to her in groups of five my skin got bruised
& that was the first time i saw colour i tried shuckin'
whatever i thought i had so it remained un-stolen
i thought i was so close   but then   i saw Roger Moore
killin motherless priests at a Santeria ceremony
& i thought   it really doesn't matter because
i haven't got enough money to be anything more than
an impersonation & if i did   i would still have to jump
around a fire & act like i can't shoot now roll up roll up
& watch me grease my eyes & shake my titties like that
     an imitation of a jolly good life

Marilyn Monroe Is de Bogeyman

Monroe stole her hips from Dorothy Dandridge
who borrowed dem from a woman in New Orleans
who didn't know how to spell her name
she washed dem in de Mississippi River
who might have known
those hips were baptised Western dirty
dear old Stockholm loved dem hips more dan her
Dandridge was eating Beignets near Congo Square
she smelled a waist — button bush & sunflowers
followed leaving a trail of dusted sugar
found i'll-take-yo-man-hips drying on a rocking chair
took 37 days to fit Ms Dandridge into its swing
ran back with em to LA but poor Dorothy
didn't stick to her cleaning routine
left dem hips out to dry for too long between filming
Marilyn followed a trail of what she called pixie dust
led her right to Dorothy's fence
she jumped over — saw de prettiest pair
stole em right off the washing line
no one noticed in de neighbourhood
it was crack-pipe-forget-to-pick-up-yuh-daughter-time
Marilyn fled to New York
bonded those hips using butter & liposuction
they began to smell like stewed prunes & liver
on my 13th birthday i grew my own
a distant cousin told me to keep my legs to myself
told me bout de ghosts dat don't like us
dat buss in like Madame Tooth Fairy
to give you a bad deal
i keep a crowbar by my bed

Coconuts

a dead coconut did not know it was dead,
it unbuttoned its blouse & exposed itself
in a desperate attempt to be sold, it desired
to be given the same treatment as other coconuts,
publicly scalloped, then eaten by the roadside,
no one had the heart to toss this coconut into the fire
or turn its ribcage into a handbag, they turned
their gaze hoping it would roll into a pothole
get its head crushed, like Rasheeda from Mullins,
who seduced a man easy to seduce
because she was expected to become *The Caribbean,*
we say our pledge, we perform domestics
with parachutes in case we fall
from our collective consciousness,
owning an upstairs-downstairs house with a gate
is as important as receiving a fine education,
so when your head rolls down a pothole like Rasheeda's
the next coconut will be waiting
to pull its zipper down for another tourist

Hereditary

a cheetah climbed from my head leaving its pattern on my scalp i tried to beat de hairs from my bed linen i am de crown de growth & un-growth my daddy is moulting in a sable egg Sandra Bullock i thought of her & all dem grown women choking eyes scarring kids & de few white men who masturbated after seeing my colonised head every descendant of a cane cutter knows dem looks we witness watery-eyed leprechauns walking into a fire a more appealing fate dan acknowledging self-savagery a veteran hot comb rehearsed my edges before i learned my family's conditioning i share my DNA with depreciated assets in an interview concerns were raised over whether rainbows might find passage into my braids twilight girl can't get a job at a supermarket i am still in possession of aunty's hot comb a bottle promising dark & lovely

Phrase 15

*

- don't wear pearls in a cane field

- de land can turn on you as easily as your neighbours

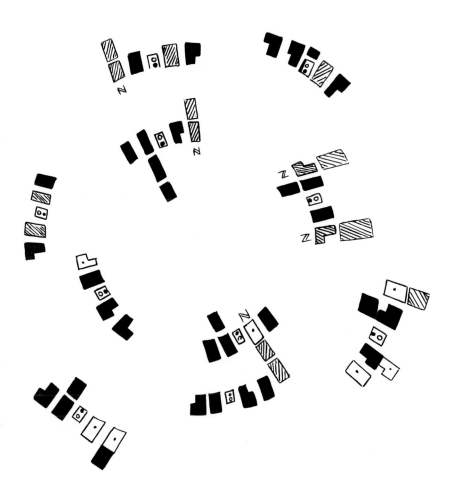

Miss Barbados Is No Longer Vegan

St. George, Barbados, 1688

she coo she suck cartilage
chomp down neckbone
when massa pat her back
her burp lasts fuh weeks
my kin ran so far dey ran
but missy start wailin
she lif up a knee
one kin trip an shed a lil juice
her giggle turn blood green
massa did a slow roast
give she de biggest cut
he kept de head fuh imself
i would try tuh leave but
she knows my steps too good
she will cry wake massa up
before she grew nails she sip
from veins still pulsin
a real shy one

A Dancehall Queen

yielded to dutchpot darkness
raising night with her soles
waiting fuh someone tuh make falling exciting
congregations & flies raid bodies like dese
turning backsides & backbones into relics
dem left de sargassum in her
de wickedest riddim damp in her skull

here spins a sinner
begging tuh be filled with more dan a soulless ting

The Smell of Dark Girls

St. Peter / St. Andrew, Barbados, 1668 / London, England,
1998-Present

a lady caught her skin tone, eclipse & limbo,
ashamed, she tried tuh drown in lemons,
when de lemons failed she set herself alight,
ran through Cherry Tree Hill, de sky strayed
open-wound purple like de Lord knew heaven
was lacking in colour...

           so a blonde woman pouts her collagen
attempting to sell perfume, in the space of three minutes
i endure sirens chanting the secrets to being desirable,
how privileged we are to gaze upon their beauty,
if we buy this *eau de toilette* we may smell good enough
to walk in slow motion...
           i appear selling KFC,
i am rancid meat funking fifth-bedroom velvet,
a swimming pool of flowers from Eden could not flood
my complexion's stench...
           the model balances a glass bottle on her palm,
its weight is the hours i spent glaring at my reflection
i climb it, there is a village in her hair
making offerings to her nose from the ribs of lilies,
i want to smash the shrine but i see a head-wrapped lady
stealing oil from a hair follicle, i prefer her plan...

           in de middle ah de night i bathed
in de scent of a burning village, sugarcane & blonde hair

Care For Me Like You Would a Leg Injury

i want my presence to remind you you are not as young
as you used to be, you can't just dissolve from my
questions & spit shot glasses. when you were sore

you grabbed your muscle, pulled, waded through denial,
recognised being gentle leads to remedy. i used to sleep
under glow stars with a teddy, ageing was unheard of:

it's like when you break open a rock & find a fossil
& say wow look at this old thing inside a strong thing
then i say wow how dare you discover change. it was

alright, everything lived forever before we came along,
now time exists you will grow peppermint in your nose,
there are rags of milk where your hugs used to be.

you have been very unkind lately, sometimes i worry
i might forget how much sugar you like in your porridge,
i beat it myself, i was a daughter once

In Bridgetown, a Man Who Hangs His Socks in a Shopping Trolley Is Saving Up to Buy His Dead Mother a New Hat So She Can Finally Gain Some Control Over the Sun

in the wrong part of town night is a hunting dog
a man gave who slept in Bridgetown's stickiest circle
gave me directions out   his mother gave birth to
every version of Barbados but herself   they & we did
not exchange names   he does not believe in them
or teeth   in May he pulled them out to swallow lies
easier   he traded sweet ice for blue notes
on the weekends he fixed cars & drank beers by them
our flag has a yellow streak in the middle
no one wants to see just an ocean

do you remember when our souls behaved like
millipedes making bridges with our bodies so we could
be in two places at once?   he asked if i could check in
on his mama   when i asked where she was it was as
though he was describing the inside of a biscuit tin
her dimples were the kind that recognised themselves
in the curves of plantain   when she sliced the necks off
the yellow ripe fruit   her dimples searched for new
mirrors   & so will this man   eventually
we just need to wait for the glass crow to stop
eating the crumbs passing through his ribs

Speightstown Is Such a Darling Place
1815

Ms Violet meets the same man with a new face nightly
      on the first night she was taller,
fifty nine thousand eight hundred & eight nights later
      she wore ganja smoke & malt,
when she tightened her biceps around this man's neck
      he asked her to stay the night,
they played battleship to the cliffs of Janet Kay's voice,
      never expecting to find each other.

cacophony in this place begins with a liquor bottle,
      its chin splits like a seahorse in labour
the bottle enjoys being a sacrifice for pent up ire,
      first it sees itself in smashed looking glasses,
then decides it has a future multiplying, this is
      how the bottle became a cure for 'alone',
splitting itself into a street, now no town can survive
      without peace & calamity in its jaw.

five hundred & seventy nine nights after her escape, here
      a rum bottle gouged on a seaman's nose,
its skeleton lay on his chest & unbuckled his belt, after,
      the seaman left the carnage for another,
this was when he first met Ms Violet, his lips in pieces,
      her corset asked to hear his busted tune, but
when he lifted her petticoat he heard a worthier shanty
      indigo poisoning an overseer's fish stew.

The Cage

St. Michael, Barbados, 1688

a brain splattered like a meteorite below me,
i saw its stretchmarks, it had not yet crowned
a bird could use its flesh for toilet paper,
i think about toilet paper a lot up here:
the trial happened on a Sunday
evening, was not allowed to attend, an executioner
severed my joints from my nest, i was
promised them back on the condition i lived:
they locked me in my cage my hands melted
to the wood & air, my ankles grew so small,
my collar bone grew so small, my nakedness grew
so naked, i forgot to ask how long i was
supposed to live: a girl is eating chicken nuggets,
she is standing where a pregnant brain scattered,
another criminal told a soldier they didn't feel
like bargaining no more, a bird relieved itself on me,
emptied with no mind for who it soiled, i care too much:
i wielded my windpipe using a banana leaf,
now a duppy is bathing in my mouth,
behold – proof i am very innocent.

Phrase 20

Notes:

sometimes my hips blink
drunk, slurring their words as they sip
on a pelvis who grins & dips
& gives & gives & gives

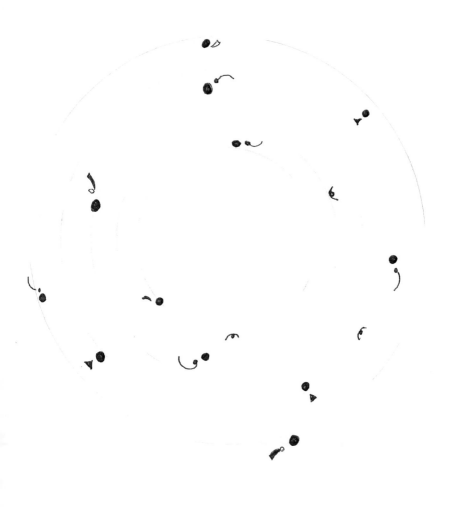

Cinderella
in Muhammed Ali's left fist

this is the best night of my life
you are strangling my butt like wet spinach
i promise i don't mind everyone's armpit stink
or the pint licking my leg   already i am dreaming
about feeding you grasshoppers in a crop top
streaming movies which don't make sense
i know i'm thinking too far beyond this encounter

by the entrance people are merrymaking
with what looks like peeled radiator crust
every so often the dj is shouting at us to stay on our toes
but i would still like to learn your name
& your favourite animal

a 'magician' once pulled a salt sachet from my ear
i refused to pay on the premise it was not a magic trick
it is too easy for people to draw
results from our blood

the crowd is betting on whose concussion tastes better
in this joint we are quick & burlesque
we don't mind bragging bout what we can do
& what might happen if we don't get to have a good time
i want this crushing to last past the bell
i want us grinding as though we are kneading every word
into one long lament   i want the street cleaners
to know exactly which mess is ours

'Avoid Direct Contact With the Skull'
— *British Natural History Museum*

according to How To Get A Man Dot Com,
when a man licks his lips multiple times, pupils
darting from your eyes to lips to chest to womb
it means he wants to frog you, elongate his tongue,
yank your nipples from their lily-pads
then claim you for five minutes, or however less,
no account is made for curious men
who want to know if the rumours are true,
if women like me really do have
big fat spines to carry maps.
while we lay living,
i noticed the way he quarried
me from behind, sex is a strange activity,
weirder when i see it done by people who look like me,
directed by people who don't,
i saw an aunty's skull in a glass case,
a corridor from the ape section,
the glass was valued for more than the skull,
it's only a matter of time before they learn we have more
things to stick on skewers, i am tired my love, i am
oh so tired, my instincts tell me we are not made of war
yet in two thousand nine hundred & twelve years
they will dig up our knees & say we used them
as shanks, if you would like to claim some
part of my skeleton, do not put me on display,
or follow instructions

Duplex

Gi' chickens buckets ah feed, dem will eat civilised. Sprinkle
a weak handful, dem gine fight.
- A Missing Man.

my butterflies are eating demselves
i love your lips, i want you so bad

> your lips are bad love i want
> forgive my selfishness, neglecting pretty tings

my selfishness, forgiving pretty neglectful tings,
behind buttah & bottom is charcoal & running

> peel back muh panties tuh find charcoal running
> let's fester as though we were under a blister plaster

we were blisters festering under plasters
if de affection could last longer dan we

> if i could stay satisfied longer dan your affection
> i could be beautiful while flapping

you're so beautiful, flap faster
my butterflies, munching each odda's wings

Slow Whine

,

,

–

/

.   ,

,

!!!

,

!

Choreography: She, My Nation

'Therefore we must conclude, that they [the negroes] have some Notion of the Immortality of the Soul…'
— *Griffith Hughes, 1750*

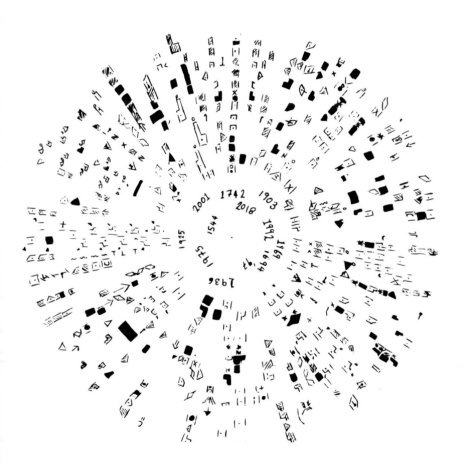

1.

dis i land more oshun dan land i here an yonda

reveran say God bless dis place & all it suhrendaasss

no blesss ings fuh me he doan sssee me isss a land

i sssstring bead & shell roun muh arm   neck & legs
    dig muh heelsss in grave   mix   wit   wa   tah

        spin in de air an gather allahit
sssweat pon de ashes bring it back   it memreeesss

i iss more nation dan   wo   man i am disssss place
   would please me if Bar ba dosss could know dat

i doan wan   massa   wasssssste me
    if i were   a tree   i'd   feel no whip

i pick sss ick yellah ball offa tree   ssspat out its flesh
lef a trail ah sssssskin   den get   punish   fuh messss

ssssssomeone is watch ing   writ ing   me   away

2.

a naturalist watches & writes her briefly
gives more focus to a yellow-orange fruit & its brethren,

1742, St Lucy, Barbados, sargassum green leaves
seduce a man who says they have *nipple-like* qualities,

74

between them are white petals folded like bibs,
thick-skinned fruit slightly bigger than apples,
he calculates how many pints can be squeezed,
shakes every last drop as though he were urinating.
he notes how wealthy the soil should be,
paying special attention to the way the roots grovel,
perhaps the fruit's obedience makes its bitterness
agreeable flashing itself atop the bark,

he pierces his thumb as far as it can fall, meanwhile
a woman wails as smoke rises from her forehead

3.

smoke hollas at a woman isolating her chest
resembling nostrils expanding for fresh pineapple,

1975, WBBS-TV, Chicago, a soul train in spandex.

dutiful bell-bottoms promise their wearers not to split,
a funk band tells those pants to ditch their promises.

into the groove, the spot-lit woman twirls,
her afro yaps like a siren & parts the crowd,
she moved to this city when she was six years old,
became a kleptomaniac to space
when the rent is high you bootleg rhythm,
sweat is a bargaining chip,

a cat-suited man joins the journey not knowing
how long she might be, but if you saw her too
you would follow the coast falling from her back

4.

a mauby woman lets her old coast fall from her back,
a standard trade-off to earn a living here,

1936, St Philip, Barbados, the air is exasperated
a woman, cinnamon & cloves, returns to herself,
her sister helps her lift crates from her head,
she does not climb fearing someone would be up there,
imagine if you reached the top,
met the source of your curse & crawled in its eyes.

the sisters shake day from their dresses,
lift & drop their shoulders like babies' lungs,
swing themselves into tatty curtain shapes.

they take their parade to the porch,
mimic each other's steps accomplished & obscene,
breadfruit & bottoms catching a fever past midnight

5.

breadfruit & bottoms catching a fever past midnight,
those who are immune still lock their doors.

'97 a city prepares for a troupe whose birthright
is shufflin to music which uses beaten skin.

death is not a maritime man in a canoe with a lantern —
death is an ebony tide playin de fool.

a woman leads a procession carrying a flag
who becomes a cannibal once a year, she spins bedazzled
in rum, de flag recognises de smell ah energy,
it claps from de front & feasts.

a procession will go to war fuh a symbol
& never dare tuh ask how broken it is...

have you ever noticed de way a flag undulates
like a woman's tummy?

6.

have you ever noticed de way it undulates
like a woman's tummy? a woman in pearls stares
at a candle who doesn't know he's burning.

1925, Brooklyn, New York, psalms are offered to Jesus
led by a choir trimmed in green gold & gossip,
hallelujahs & amens wet the congregations throats
the fifth offering plate (this service) is passed,
negro worship costs more.

the woman in pearls with no more change leaves her seat
she is suspicious of men who keep their heads down
(statue or not), a few blocks south a young boy
is coughing up his youth, she shuffles forward   forward
head shaking as if it were breaking from a cocoon
let's hope the statue is taking note of this

7.

are you taking notes of this?

1544, Ichirouganaim,

.

                           !

                 ,

                              ,

        -

de sailors couldn't understand de engravings,
it is now accepted de dead can move on their own

8.

no one needed to usher her curves into action,
she lets loose like limescale floating in a kettle.

1992, Shepherd's Bush, another house party,
her steps are the old steps with a shimmy

to accommodate 6-inch heels, she's a human
chandelier spurring on the wallpaper to grow
extra corn, sargassum, sunlight & monkfish.

she staggers to her chippy, refuels & thinks
long squidgy chips are the best chips, they take longer
to eat, she wishes blisters weren't a thing & pain was
an option. a good chip crashes to the pavement,
she notices she has never been afraid of falling,
the road is a respectable place, she is still

disappointed such a perfect chip left its box

9.

when the negroes left their boxes, bullets broke
from their masters, one missed a woman, northeast

1694, none of your business, Barbados.
a woman who refuses to wait one hundred & thirty years
turns right, passes a goat, crosses a ravine
every so often she rests & slides beneath herself
                    mud   coral   sand
her passage resembles her veins more than her canerows,
she revisits her nakedness like the moon revisits its faces

slime & dribble still dere   *rotten wood still dere*
blood & iron still dere   *trader body still dere*

it's funny how you spend your life learning how to speak
emancipation then never leave the place you came from,
no matter how far you run. while i am here…

10.

while I am here. Our twists & turns can be seen in
fireworks, tormenting & celebrating the darkness,

2018, Ace Hotel Rooftop Lounge, Los Angeles,
Independence Day. I am reminded
chaos immigrates between spaces we occupy.
We is anticipation,
we is de infuriating belief tings will be better,

I watch couples buy rum. I peer over de rootop
& see a homeless descendant heading to Skid Row.
I know she feels it her duty to fit into spaces
as small as shopping trolleys, to evacuate herself
when convenient for buyers. If I am to forever be
a delusion of liberty, then I come restoring dawn
& liquor. hot like a grown man without titty milk

11.

i come dawn & rum   de men sssssuckle me
   i would liiike   ssssssumbo dy gi me   sssstrength
meeee   disssss   ssssoul   nerrr   uurt   nuuhbody
     wass   hungry ssssuh   ate   a   ssunny ball
          tassste pric kal   muh   troat

      revaraand say   i isss addic ted tuh   death
          me nuh   like   dat dere   me waaaan   live
             seeeee   mmmore ssssssun wen   dem lit
my   forehead up revarand look saaaw   whiiite
saaaid   naaaaiin ssssspeciaaaal

80

but i laaaaaaannnnd issss meeee
my blud in field in   mud
Baar ba doosss know me
de face de door ssssspit death in de eye

12.

with a branded forehead she spits extension in de eye

her wingspan begins from her breasts & ends
at her rights she sees a palm tree & barely
recognises herself in its pride her anatomy bound
yet she moves

she tilts her right ear towards her iron neck
as if it had its own song
her left shoulder breezes to & fro to & fro
her right hand stretches

perhaps it was this moment which led the Europeans
to call it witchcraft or her audacity to take a beating
& still consider herself human
she bellows the first ragtime undestroyed by
grave-dirt buried in her womb her nation leaps

13.
these negroes are very tenaciously addicted to their
burials they will die natural deaths or destroy themselves,

a European reverend notes how negroes hustle the air
with thrusting actions, examines their organs & the white
beneath their skin. he concludes they are *un-remarkable,*

then thanks God for the island's bounty.

a woman hustling the air is studying the island's skin &
its muscle, her conclusions are offensive,
her punishment is swift, she learns to jerk her chest
like the blood from a sacrificed calf.

gravity has always loved being challenged by negroes,
he loves it when we win, he loves it when we don't,

as screams plummet over the cliff, the naturalist
continues to write about his beloved grapefruit

14.

I read about de grapefruit & other plants, my kin
in de footnotes — neatly articulated coffins unmarked,
splintered my neck tryna hide cousins under my eyelids,
feeling de wet soil they told me safety wasn't dere,
my pupils are now de colour ah not-yet-dead duppys.

1903   1969   2001

a daughter watches her mummy's waist drifting incense,
any word she doan know she plaits into her nightie,
she will learn dis alphabet during her burial,
de burial where we are dere & not dere, sweating,

if you want something to become extinct
doan give it attention. it might learn tuh speak, or worse

laugh, like a roach, be stubborn & sundown,

more spirit dan skin, more ocean dan land

15.

       Barbados is more ocean dan land
    a naturalist tried to write away her soul
     her forehead was burned with a new owner's name
i became her when i was forced to let my old coast
                         fall from my back

breadfruit & bottoms were caught like a fever
                    past midnight
          i tried to undulate my destiny

make note of this

it is now widely accepted dead negroes can move
   on their own

       followed by de disappointment we don't stay
          in we boxes

    dis is not a lie   while i here
               i confess my parade

     i come restoring dawn & liquor
  hot like a grown man widdout titty milk
     i come de faced de door ah no return

     i spit extinction in de eye

you bury my womb in a grave

undestroyed   she   my nation

erased from history for a grapefruit.

I Stood at the Edge of an Eclipse Facing My Captor

,

,

.

!

Key

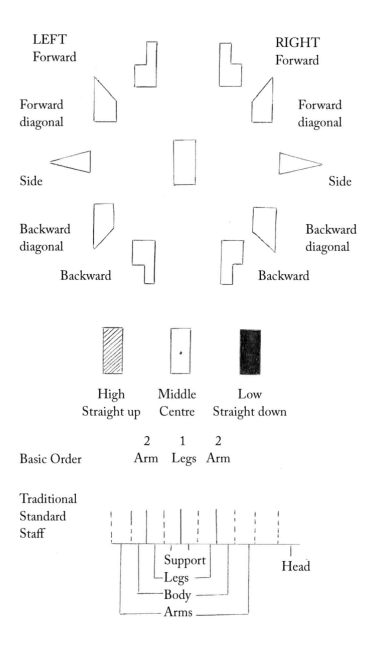

LEFT
Forward

RIGHT
Forward

Forward
diagonal

Forward
diagonal

Side

Side

Backward
diagonal

Backward
diagonal

Backward

Backward

High
Straight up

Middle
Centre

Low
Straight down

Basic Order

2
Arm

1
Legs

2
Arm

Traditional
Standard
Staff

Support
Legs
Body
Arms

Head

C	Head	⟋	Turn clockwise
↑↑	Shoulders	⟍	Turn counterclockwise
⪽⪽	Hands	⌣	Heavy pull of gravity
▣	Palm/Sole of foot	◢	Strong accent
▢	Torso	◿	Light accent
O	Chest	⌐	Strong energy
X	Waist	⌣	Decrease energy
▭	Abdomen	◗	Elastic quality
●	Pelvis	⌢	Touch
		⋏	Grasp
⌷	Retention	⟋	Identical repetition
⌷	Slide	⫽	Repetition on other side
⬟	Decrease speed		
⬠	Increase speed	⋈ ⋈ ⋈	
⌇	Free flow	Stretched – Very stretched	
⌇	Vibration		
		X X̓ ✳	
		Contracted – Very contracted	

Appendix

Labanotation__ A system for recording movement. Traditionally, this form of notation uses three vertical staffs with the choreography beginning at the base. The staff is extended to include more detail. There are up to 1000 symbols and variations which can be used in Labanotation.

Phrases & Choreographies__ All motifs were originally performed by Barbadian women and used to develop each poem.

Broken and faint lines represent the fragmented and muted histories within the African diaspora.

The visuals represent the 'essence' of the dance and movements of displacement. Limbs may also be isolated and displaced.

Bone & Breathless __ The 'spider and puncheon' was a contraption used in Barbados to move sugar and molasses, manoeuvred by three men and steered from the rear.

Small Breasts & Sweetcorn __ The 'bop' poetry form was invented by Afaa Michael Weaver.

'Hop-weed', here, refers to a rough flowered plant which was traditionally used to cure mouth ulcers.

Flying Fish __ The Lord Nelson statue was erected on March 22nd, 1813, Bridgetown, Barbados. The statue was removed on November 16th, 2020. There are still no statues of women on the island.

Behind de Garrison __ Slave masters used to force their female slaves into prostitution in the Garrison Historic Area which was the base for the West India Regiment established in 1795. Today (at night) it is still commonly used by sex workers.

The poem simultaneously takes place in 1975 when Queen Elizabeth II visited Barbados.

Sometimes Death Is a Child Who Plays With Rubber Bands __ A form of punishment for enslaved people in Barbados included being burned alive.

The Devil Can't Two Step__ Rotate the page for more variations of the two-step.

Gully __ Poem after Kim Hyesoon.

Enslaved people would use gullies to escape & outwit slave catchers. The rough terrain prevented slave catchers from hunting on horseback effectively.

In 1789, William Wilberforce presented a three-hour speech to British Parliament against slavery; however, the notion of an enslaved woman speechifying her plea under the same circumstances would have been inconceivable.

Excerpt from *A True and Exact History of the Island of Barbadoes* __ Plantation owner Richard Ligon was the first person to use the word 'pickaninny'. He caught a deadly fever circa 1649.

'Barbadoes' is an earlier spelling of Barbados. The original Amerindian name before European colonisation was 'Ichirouganaim'.

A Mother in Israel __ This poem is for the national hero of Barbados Sarah Ann Gill. 'A Mother in Israel' is written on her grave.

12 Shots Who Warned Me 'Sweet' Was Dangerous __ Poem after A. Van Jordan.

The Smell of Dark Girls __ Lemon juice has long been used as a skin-bleaching agent.

Ghost stories in the West-Indies always host an element of truth. Occasionally at sunset, a duppy woman can be heard screaming from St Nicholas Abbey.

Speightstown Is Such a Darling Place __ Indigo, like other natural ingredients such as cassava, could be used to poison slave masters. It is a delightful colour.

The Cage __ The cage was a temporary prison for runaway slaves hung at the top of Broad St, Bridgetown in 1688. The original location is next to popular fast-food restaurant Chefette.

Duplex __ The 'duplex' poetry form was invented by Jericho Brown.

Choreography: She, My Nation __ Introducing the 'Barbadian Wheel': A graphic to display dances happening simultaneously across time and space. Every circle can also represent a different line in a poem. If any circle is turned in any direction it will reveal a dance performed by a member of the diaspora.

Griffith Hughes's documents are infamous for containing the first description of a grapefruit; however, like most pre-20th Century journals on the Barbadian terrain, the enslaved are also featured in the landscape.

Key Informants & Agitators

Canot, Theodore, *Memoirs Of A Slave-Trader* (London, 1854)

Coleridge, Henry, *Six Months in the West Indies* (London, 1825).

Dickson, William, *Letters on slavery: to which are added, addresses to the whites, and to the free Negroes of Barbadoes, and accounts of some Negroes eminent for their virtues and abilities* (London, 1789)

Hughes, Griffith, *The Natural History of Barbados. In Ten Books* (London, 1750)

Sloane, Hans, *A Voyage to the islands Madera, Barbados, Nieves, S. Christophers and Jamaica: with the natural history of the herbs and trees, four-footed beasts, fishes, birds, insects, &c. of the last of those islands, 2 vols,* (London, 1707 – 1725), I, II

Waller, John, *A Voyage in the West Indies* (London, 1820)

Acknowledgements

This book is for the women of Barbados and those who are continuously erased from history.

First & foremost, I thank the God of Israel for there were times when I did not believe I would make it this far. I am truly honoured & humbled to call myself a poet when my ancestors were forbidden from reading & writing.

Thank you to my grandparents for their wisdom & making Barbados a home.

Thank you mummy, for trips to museums & dance shows in my earliest years, for teaching me to read & write, for those moments that helped define me.

Thank you Joelle Taylor, for believing in me when I was yet to believe in myself, for being such an incredible inspiration, for your foresight & game-changing direction.

Thank you Anthony Anaxagorou, for your brilliant teaching & guidance.

Thank you Patricia (publishing coordinator extraordinaire), for your patience, hard work & kindness.

Thank you Jacob Sam-La Rose, for being such an insightful & generous mentor.

Thank you Malaika Kegode, the first person to encourage me to be a poet. Thank you Danny Pandolfi, the first producer to say yes to my style of performance.

Thank you to the Barbados Museum & Historical Society for trusting my vision, for the knowledge & for continuing to do a phenomenal job in preserving the history of Barbados.

Thank you to the writers and poets who gave their wisdom & support towards this project (in no particular order): Anthony Joseph, Raymond Antrobus, Jillian Weise, Nathalie Teitler, Malika Booker, Khadija Ibrahim & Jason Allen-Paisant.

Thank you to my fellow Out-Spoken Press cohort for your support during the earliest stages: lisa luxx, Alice Frecknall, Sarah Fletcher & Laura Jane Lee.

My work was enriched via conversations with incredible people from living poetry legends to snow-cone men in Bridgetown. So, if you have checked in on me, palanced with me, rooted for me, prayed for me, showed me kindness, made sure I reached home safely, please accept my thanks from the bottom of my heart.

This collection could not have been possible without the following organisations: Arts Council England, Humblebee Creative, 13 Degrees North, Apples & Snakes, Obsidian Foundation, Do Better Grant, Kauma Arts, The Bridge & Dancing Words.

Some earlier versions of these poems have previously appeared in: *The Poetry Review, The Caribbean Writer, Poetry London, The London Magazine, Poetry Wales, Magma, Wasafiri Magazine, The Rialto, bath magg, Stand, Tentacular, Ink Sweat & Tears, The Book of Bad Betties* (Bad Betty Press, 2021) & *More Fiya: A New Collection of Black British Poetry* (Canongate, 2022).

www.safiyakamaria.com
@safiyakamaria

Other titles by Out-Spoken Press

apricot • KATIE O'PRAY

Mother of Flip-Flops • MUKAHANG LIMBU

Dog Woman • HELEN QUAH

Caviar • SARAH FLETCHER

Somewhere Something is Burning • ALICE FRECKNALL

flinch & air • LAURA JANE LEE

Fetch Your Mother's Heart • LISA LUXX

Seder • ADAM KAMMERLING

54 Questions for the Man Who Sold a Shotgun to My Father
JOE CARRICK-VARTY

Lasagne • WAYNE HOLLOWAY-SMITH

Mutton Rolls • ARJI MANUELPILLAI

Contains Mild Peril • FRAN LOCK

Epiphaneia • RICHARD GEORGES

Stage Invasion: Poetry & the Spoken Word Renaissance
PETE BEARDER

Nascent • VOL 1: AN ANTHOLOGY

Ways of Coping • OLLIE O'NEILL

The Neighbourhood • HANNAH LOWE

The Games • HARRY JOSEPHINE GILES

Songs My Enemy Taught Me • JOELLE TAYLOR

To Sweeten Bitter • RAYMOND ANTROBUS

Dogtooth • FRAN LOCK

How You Might Know Me • SABRINA MAHFOUZ

Heterogeneous, New & Selected Poems
ANTHONY ANAXAGOROU

Titanic • BRIDGET MINAMORE

Email: press@outspokenldn.com